NO MOON

NO MOON

Nancy Eimers

PURDUE UNIVERSITY PRESS / WEST LAFAYETTE, INDIANA

01 00 99 98 97   5 4 3 2 1

The paper used in this book meets the minimum requirements
of American National Standard for Information Sciences—
Permanence of Paper for Printed Library Materials, ANSI Z39.48-1992.
♾™

Printed in the United States of America
Design by inari

Library of Congress Cataloging-in-Publication Data
Eimers, Nancy.
        No moon / Nancy Eimers.
        p. cm.
        ISBN 1-55753-099-8 (pbk. : alk. paper)
        I. Title
PS3555.I46N6 1997
811'.54—dc21   96-45290
                                        CIP

Acknowledgment is made to the following periodicals, where some of the poems appeared, sometimes in different versions:

Alaska Quarterly: "A Night without Stars," "No Moon"
Crab Orchard Review: "Autistic Twins at the Fireworks"
Crazyhorse: "Born Worrier," "Lakes"
Indiana Review: "World of Tomorrow"
Michigan Quarterly Review: "Unplugged"
North American Review: "The Pelican Girl"
Paris Review: "Joy to the World," "On the Phone with My Parents"
Prairie Schooner: "Betty and Joe"
Poetry Northwest: "Absent Bird Moon," "Everlastings," "A History of Navigation," "In the New Year," "Of the Constellation Perseus"
TriQuarterly: "The Match Girl," "Old Things," "Outer Space," "Space Life"

"A History of Navigation" and "A Night without Stars" were reprinted in *The Best American Poetry 1996*, edited by Adrienne Rich (New York: Scribner).

I'd like to thank Rich Lyons, Susan Prospere, Alane Rollings, and David Wojahn for their help and encouragement. Special thanks to Bill Olsen.

for my mother and father

CONTENTS

IV.

I

OUTER SPACE

Today I caught the feeling-tone of a voice on the street, though
   not the words—

someone was asking a question
of the silence and of the waiting

that live in things suburban and stationary:
windows, garage doors, sidewalks, unlit streetlights,
the bland topography of the lawns.

This was a daylight question,

not one you'd ask of glimmer or flight,
lit streetlights, star magnitudes, fireflies, TV snow.

Not the moonless night question
you'd ask of flowering bulbs
and vegetables that bear their crops below the ground.

Not a question that drives you out of Self
like a moth to its porch-light epipsychidion

but a question that drives you into Self
like the soul of a rock in torrential rains.

Not the question a roadside diner asks
of its empty parking lot.
Nothing a shadow could ask of a highway underpass.

This was a question mouthed by a man

not by the drone of an edger,
not by the blown trees gliding into place.
Not by the ants that follow their winding scent-paths through
   the blades of grass.

Asked by the visible, asked by the working lips and tongue.

What sounds and moves
was asking its question of what does not,

something to do with the peeling paint on the walls
and the crooked pitch of the roofs, the dampness creeping into
   the cinderblock basements

and soaking down the chimney flashings,
the festering of the gutters, the glandular swell of the wood,
the rust that lines the pipes that, linked together, would reach
   to outer space.

I don't remember an answering—

just the vertigo of ascent, just the looking over a cliff
that is any question.

The street didn't know there was anything wrong
with its shingles, flashings, sockets, anthills,
deferrals, lulls.

I heard the sound slide out of its words.
Not a full-moon question asked of the windows that gorge
on the magnitudes of the stars

but a lifting up of a human voice
that could not lie and could not promise to lift us
out of disrepair

or lift us in our waiting out of what we are waiting for.

UNPLUGGED

To live inside was the simple first idea behind a house:
a noun
but soft inside. Lined by down.
My husband is playing Nirvana *Unplugged,*
Cobain's wail, stripped down to the wood,
is wood—wild, mad—
akin to the Germanic *Wut,* for "rage."
His "In the Pines" so bare
each unplugged guitar's a door
slammed home.
And then, a little while,
all softnesses that line a human nest
are gone: low voices, the velvet art
of sleeping faces, long breaths to sleep
and the long breaths back again.
Home gone down.
In the pines, in the pines, where the sun don't ever shine.
Jesus, they're fighting again.
Who? I don't know, everybody, everybody.
The woman and man in the song,
my husband and me.
Sometimes,
next door a father shouts at his son, thirteen,
who sobs tightly from the frail shoulders all the way down.
Wood mad. Ready to clobber
his bigger father. *Oh yeah. As if.*
To live inside a tidy box: wasn't that the idea?
I will shiver . . . and the trees have snuck
out of their skeletons again, it's late,
the khaki green of a house across the street
spills from its military square

the whole night through.
In the bluegrass version, Bill Monroe's high whine
mimics the blue-and-gray edges
of wind sawing back and forth in the deepening
graygreen pines;
but Cobain's is all black shriek. An act of erasure.
Someone is rubbing the paper hard . . .
lead bleeds, the paper tears. No color for that.
My girl, my girl, don't lie to me —
a soft black wind
is rubbing out *her* part in the song. Poor little girl. She has no home.
She has no voice
but the pines.
The common nighthawk lays its eggs on a gravel roof,
no nest —
the killdeer burrows in a cinder bed, its eggs are
spotted, scrawled on, blotched buff-and-black
to look like trash.
I'm going where the cold wind blows.
Who says that? — no one says that
mouthless howl.
Where are we going?
Unplug the lights in the houses,
what becomes of us? Killdeer may even nest in broken glass
between the ties of railroad tracks still in use,
but we —
unplug our houses, and how dark
do we become?
I can hear the neighbor boy still sobbing
madly onto the breast of the family station wagon.

A HISTORY OF NAVIGATION

1. Insomnia

Awake at midnight on the factory side of town,
I swear the only thing I haven't tried

is counting ships. The *Water Witch*, the *Golden Fleece*,
the *Silver Wake*, the *Sailor Boy*, the *Morning Star*,

and last, the *Kalamazoo*. I made that up. This shipwrecked town—
I can almost *see* its rooftops fathoms down.

I think the starless night is trying to push
right through the walls of this house.

So is the screaming train en route through our backyard
with a load of dark that would fill Lake Michigan.

Street light pours through a flowering rent
on a sheet that curtains our bedroom window;

my sleeping husband is another window
dark for hours now, and I am watching him,

too far out to care for signs and omens:
the traffic light blinks red and red and red;

the Minute Market, lit inside, shuts off.
I call it Murder Market; someone was shot there once.

How can he sleep through the dirty sound?
Garage bands never sleep. The singer's voice

is husky, dragged through mud.
Just one way to tell a love story.

Not our story, in particular,
or his. The story of an open mouth.

*

Mouth open, breathing quietly,
you seem to skim over the water, as a ship does.
How can you sleep?
Halfway down the street, a man is laughing,
so hard I think he'll empty out,
but no, the laugh goes on.
It just gets fainter down the street.
Once the last remembered house blinks out,
it's all dead reckoning,
whimsy or currents, wind, a lazy minute hand
as I think my way past any hope of sleep.
This afternoon—what was I screaming right into your eyes?
Poor Richard's Diner down the street
will be dark until morning, ages away,
though in my mind I am already groping
for landmarks:

Oh red and blue tower of Statler Cement,
Kozel Iron & Metal, oh Dairy Mart,
oh corner of Crosstown Parkway and Mill
with your two orange newspaper machines,
the Detroit Free Press and the Kalamazoo Gazette—
my mind is newsprint letters cut out of a page of night.
Will things we said leave holes in our morning and afternoon?

2. The Worst Fight in Our History

After a squall, on the beach from Ludington
to Sleeping Bear Point,
the breakers push and drag ashore
the timbers to a hundred ancient wrecks.
Floating stairways. A stove-in pilot house.

When the part of us that feels most alive
rises through the fathoms of the argument,
we look around, we ask how far
our voices carry us.

Did the neighbors hear?
Your face empties out like a room for rent.

February 4: auspicious day for marriage
and repair of ships.

What can we do for each other? Out the window,
across the oceanic lawn
I see a neighbor turning busily away
from the mouth of our quiet
to *his* lawn and *his* flower bed and *his* house and *his* quiet—

*

—after the age of schooners, after the age of steamers,
after the walking-beam engine and the paddle wheel
with good power on the downstroke

but not much on the up,
in the sickening lunges of smoke and pause,
how can anyone have much of an appetite?

But everyone seems to be ravenous.
In the morning a diner is mostly men and smoke,
men who blow out smoke in stale blossomings,

blue anchors, stale hearts drifting apart—
men whose stares dribble nowhere.
How many ages ago did I see a face as if through wavy glass?

What day was it, what time, whose face?

I want to make a date with your sleeping face.
Tomorrow morning. You and me
over greasy eggs and American fries.
We'll tell our dreams,
though probably not quite *to* each other's eyes.
Let each one sail his lack of narrative
as if there were a port
in all that fog.
Or will I have slept enough to dream?
Sleepless nights blink red in the window,
morning is an empty parking lot.

I want to ask your face across the fish tank of a booth:
whose name is advertised on the coffee cups
floating toward us on a tray?
Is it yours or mine?

Which one of us is Kozel, Statler, Crosstown, Mill?
Poor Richard will be wiping the counter
the way he always does,
between the booths there will be those troughs
where it gets all quiet
after the gale wind blows
for the early shift. Across the silences
of dollar bills tucked under plates
I will remember this
dream about owls up in the trees.
They are screeching
here I am.

3. A History of Navigation

Sometimes in a squall
the pouring of storm oil on the water
doesn't work. Then the wind goes whistling
over the forty- and fifty-foot crests
and the gloomy cook goes sloshing around in the ship's galley
stacking pots and pans on the highest shelf.
Each time
we turn the volume up, then down, behind the words,
we weep, we make of sweet relief our peace,
we scan the windows for superlatives: *One of the most daring
pieces of expert seamanship
in the history of navigation!*
To voyage over water, to make our way—
let's lie in bed in the hour of shipwrecked laughs,
one awake and one asleep,
and steer past the first or last
jalopy backfiring in the alley.

Poor car, poor town,
roar down inside us and sleep.

SPACE LIFE

for Lynda Schraufnagel, in memory

Back in our Houston neighborhood was a wall of graffiti
signed at the bottom,
by Space Life, Low Life, Scared Life, Feeble Life,
each poor ghost out there with its whispering
spray-paint can while night crept over the firmament
of the ceiling lamp and roaches went swarming away
into cracks and cabinets, under the drainboard, down the drain,
as if they didn't want to be wished on.
I could almost hear roaches multiplying inside the walls,
I could almost hear the fuzzy stars and the yellow sawhorse light
blinking all night in the street to slow night down.
I'd stand in the dark and run the COLD tap,
never very cold, tunnel of water erasing the glass in my hand,
erasing my mouth . . .
one morning I found a syringe dropped in the grass
and bent to look, and not even touching it left a rubbing sensation
between my finger and thumb, invisible envelope
addressed to time or light or whatever dark
the windows shrugged off busily between supper and midnight,
one after another. *I was so bad,* you'd say—
a way you spoke, an emphasis so droll
I hear it now, exactly, how you stress the *so*—
and I'd envy you, who always got there first,
envy you all the way back to a moment I cradled
a '60s op art notebook, trying to figure out
if the rippling squares on the cover were coming or going
while you were already doing both,
you were a high-school girl already wild somewhere,
each day, briefly, you were a bank teller with middle-aged women

nice to you in spite of your lips' unearthly whitish gloss
and the nipples budding hard beneath your lime green minidress.
And later, in Paris, you with a lover,
half-awake over coffee, lifting the cup, knowing just enough
to say *encore* to the waitress. On the canceled
ticket of that word I'd travel down our street
to the steps of the Houston apartment house
where I lived with my boyfriend in student poverty.
I can feel the windows across the street
reserving their judgment,
"Gimme Shelter" drifting out of one or maybe
all of them. I remember they wouldn't quite stare
at a pasty-faced man in pajama top and jeans who dragged
his hips along, pushing a grocery cart of empties
that rattled together like all of his bones.
When he lifted a bottle-shaped bag to his mouth,
I had to look away,
oh lips and tongue the doors of breath and saliva—
enough! enough! a radio blares
and you are gone from a Houston spring already hot as summer,
each last chaste magnolia blossom is doddering open
and nothing is more or less than a breath.
By the time I traveled to the broken metropolis
of a Paris graveyard and saw the grave of Jim Morrison,
it was only a concrete slab
with *Jim* scratched everywhere with scissors or bobby pin.
I swear a teenaged boy was perched there
drinking wine, messenger angel
bored with his immaculate message: *he is not here.*
The painted marble head on the tombstone was gone, too—stolen.
So this boy holds out the jug; then my fingers are reaching

to cradle it there in the formal wreckage,
yes, this is it all right, just this,
to disappear for a second between my fingers and his.
Sometimes your voice drifts over an otherwise
still afternoon, and it is the voice of Jim Morrison
like a droopy voluptuous flower, opening
to find out if there's breath or sleep at the end of the line.
I can't even tell which window it's coming from, or which flower,
I can't even scream at it to shut it up, I don't
live on that street anymore.

BETTY AND JOE

When a month has two full moons, the second is blue,
but the first is ordinary,
shining tonight at the top of Stone Avenue
like one working headlight,
and whoever or whatever steers the invisible wheel
has not decided where to go after work, in the idle hours:
drive home to one of the little adobes
or stop at Kim's Spice Rack, or maybe visit the tar-paper shack
where a man is lying against the chain-link fence.
And when my husband and I hold out our hands
to hoist him up, he's sweet and sorry
and mumbles like he's our fallen son:
I did something bad. I drank.
Inside the door of the shack
piles of crumpled donut bags make airy mountains.
They sigh out when we lower him down to sleep
the sleep of the vases and unwound clocks and feathered fans
tarpaulin-covered at night at the neighbor's perpetual yard sale:
humps of gray like snowfall
when at dawn I barely wake and look out through
our bleary windows just to be purely alone for a second,
then falling asleep among all the other seconds.
The moon by then has dissolved
in a tallboy left half-full on the fence.
Last night the cats made hurt little hooked sounds
until we let them out. Tonight Betty tells me
the next time her husband Joe catches Lemon
pawing through their garbage he'll shoot him dead.
There's a Blue Moon Bar, where he drinks with his friends
    from the factory.

And the Blue Moon Construction Company is roofing a house
    on Helen Street.
One of the roofers told Betty *that husband of yours*
is a lucky guy. Now she haunts him,
hauling her baby past the house like a sack of potatoes,
wallowing in the echo of hammering loosed from the hammer
as the moon slips under the shiny fingernail
on her baby's moist thumb.
I used to tell her how young she looked
until I found out she was only twenty-two.
Then what was there to say,
what to do with all the straight pins she picked from our carpet,
the wads of stuffing that leak from holes in the couch—
clawed by one of the cats in labor,
frantic to find a place alone enough to birth in.
When the month is over,
what to do when the blue moon asks us out
past the squalling of Little Joe
and the crack of cue on ball at the Spice Rack,
asks us into the ache of my womb,
soft as the neon letters glowing over the bar,
and before we know it, the moon
that doesn't love anyone has taken something
ordinary away from us again.

NO MOON

Now it's a way of remembering, dark by dark, the rows.
To think my way back to that rising full harvest moon

is to set in more winter firewood, for it will be cold.

To look at that moon is secretly to make a purchase
for no good reason, of old watch faces in bulk,

is to trace the trajectory of a mayfly on its slow crawl

across the splotched ephemeris of a tablecloth
from points *everlasting* to *dead at the end of a day.*

To look at the moon is to open up little bottles and boxes,

beach glass, blue jay feather, clearies, cat's-eyes,
heart of a hummingbird, snowdrift, fingernails, rain,

until it breaks, it drips, it melts, it rots, it stinks of camphor,

it lies, it doesn't tell.
At dusk, the moon is low in the south

and nearing the Teapot in the constellation Sagittarius

as we travel eastward against the stars.
Each night this week the moon will wax in cosmic reverie. Not yet.

A crow flying cleanly over the houses

has the hardness of trees, or is it the houses
drawing near like trees in the sooty light

that keeps the very thought of us alive?

Down a road outside town I remember *silhouette trees*
and every silhouette giving in.

The moon rose over dinosaurial waddlings

of Canada geese between the cornstalk rows
as if the almanac had told it just what to do:

corn carried, let such as be poor go and glean.

WORLD OF TOMORROW

What the hollow sound is, what it belongs to
has something to do with a train's immensity
rushing out of us.

And the whistle belongs to our own insatiable tracks
curving out of sight, as the tracks belong to the point at which
this town will disappear. The towns belong

to the thread they are strung on,
dank bars and birdcage barns on the outskirts of our saying goodbye
belong to the suitcases which belong

to the matching garment bags folded soundlessly into themselves
which in turn belong to the dust each passenger's grip
shucks off when he lifts his hand, goodbye, hello,

and the shucked-off mites of dust
form a hand that rides its curve of air
from a thread of hair to an eyelash tip.

And we belong, and every single mite of dust.

I like to be rushed out of my dust
by a moving train and I like to be left behind
as immensity drops sparrow feathers

between the tracks. To feel the train rush out of me,
to be static, to walk these railroad ties back
and to be the town not going anywhere.

To be inside a body that's going to go
is not so bad. A train rushes out of a station
and by the time it's gone around the bend

that town is a tiny abandoned World of Tomorrow.
Passengers looking out of the train
see the windows of warehouses are the slots in a penny arcade

and they tell time by the clock face of every house.
Steel springs coil inside the trees.
Then the train will pull them down the tracks

they can't invent fast enough for their need to survive.

IN THE NEW YEAR

. . . all the different suns the material galaxies
will form out of, the little bright spots that are
galaxies. . . . If something ends, still, how
infinitely much there is that isn't ending!
                              —Randall Jarrell, letter

For L. S.

In Baghdad, they fly up, little bright spots
to find and marry the bombs falling down,

and they are not the stars on childhood's bedroom wall
that wake when it's dark enough and shine on us,

and hoard the thought
of a million suns as the soul travels nightly

through constellations behind the stars,
each pinning a layer of dark in place.

And they are not van Gogh's pinwheeling stars.
Sleep fizzles out above our heads,

flinging itself out of any night
we ever found the terror to go on looking at.

Has the thought of you already forgotten us?
Last week a CBS reporter and camera crew

abandoned their jeep and wandered into the Saudi desert,
beyond our knowledge, beyond their own—

that's what you've come to, that's where you are.
Not even to know there's a war!

Yet, as friends do, I keep wanting to tell you
what you already know. I mean the empty

imagining. A kid flies one of those dark spots
over the city and lets it drop,

a diamond flicked out of a ring,
then rides on a bezel, emptied, back toward base;

he is looking down like a greater darkness
hosting what another kid-pilot called "the greatest

Fourth of July bash ever!"
and thinking what he mustn't ever think.

Stars burning on the ground,
millions of suns and their planets, smoking, spent . . . .

In Kalamazoo it is snowing eternally
like notes on the roll of a player piano,

the nobody playing what nobody always plays:
where are you? why aren't you here?

In my mind I keep circling around
to find my footsteps waiting, pressed in snow.

In a recent movie a man is staring at *Crows in a Wheatfield* so intently
he walks in and out of the bright shafts of light.

Inside, sheaves of it are already heaped and bound.
But sooner or later he's drawn irresistibly

to his body's own impatience
waiting just outside the idea of art. Nothing stops

the tiny, flickering TV war I watch in a darkened room.
Each smack of light that pilots me back to myself

flicks my eyes shut just before the night
isn't you anymore. It is everything else.

THE MATCH GIRL

Did you know a poor girl in a fairy tale has to fall asleep
   in the bitterest cold on earth just to wake up
  in the garden of heaven? I had to die to warm my hands
which were blue and cold with the journey,

   had to cup their frozen wastes
  to the bluest flowers, lupine, delphinium and the Blue Skies petunia
so the glacial melt at my fingertips
   could begin. By then the eons of smoke from my matches

  had cauterized my nostrils and lungs
so I couldn't smell even the loudest
   of heaven's flowers—the salvia
  making such ruckus and stink with its red

that a million hummingbirds trembled into its ruffled sleeves.
   But my ears being for no reason heavenly now,
  I heard the million-and-first one splashing thunderously
in the water pooled on a lily pad.

   And the red-hot poker burned all day
  in case the night should return,
though it never will, though all the time I think of asking it.
   This little light of mine . . .

  guttered out in my fingers. I probably *blew* it out.
Then was it a shooting star I rode from earth
   to the lowest rung of the dark and looked down
  at the skyline—

I could FEEL the buildings shaken down to their girders,
        HEAR the loosening nuts and bolts . . . as now I taste
    the nectar pumped along these dumb beseeching tongues.
The earth below seemed blue inside

        like an empty milk of magnesia bottle—
    used up, rinsed and dried, set out on a windowsill.
I want to ask if we remember long
        but I KNOW. The page will turn.

    This little punk with smudgy eyes and hands,
who, even as she was doing it, vaguely remembered peeling matches
        out of the book of the dark,
    striking them one by one against a wall

in a burning graffiti that ate itself up
        or was eaten by breath,
    will forget. The skyline. The Gold Star Chili sign.
The jitter and blink from the Shooting Star.

for Lynda Hull

LIVE OAKS

These nerve-end trees hung over us with a dread
whose musings were a thousand layers deep,
a billion pursed leaves sucking in dioxides
while Spanish moss, hung in corkscrewing strands,
repeated lies. All lies. Still we walked here
most nights, down the red brick path
that promised a fairy tale under the trees
if we listened hard enough, told us night
was a slowly turning page, and day was a drunk
crashed out on the other side, in Bell Park, belly up
to a drift of roses, car exhaust, McDonald's fries,
that was how the oak trees saw our lives.
Promised there'd be trouble all along the way,
parceled out by these houses, castles really,
wedding cake balconies with iron froth,
strident daylilies, electric fences, a Doberman
with a bark like a tomahawk nipping at our heels.
In that house a witch lived—see the tower,
salmon pink adobe, where she let down her pitch black hair,
but no one climbed at midnight, no one . . .
see where the dogs with eyes as big as millstones
lunged at the ornamental wishing well
a drunk crawled into with his bottle, crooning to it.
And in the gutter, islanded with newspaper and Kleenex
are the burnt matchsticks and crumpled cigarettes
the little Match Girl lit one night and held
against the bottoms of her feet, until the cops arrived
and hauled her off. Somebody's version of heaven
must be drawing us out at night, or maybe what draws us
is the way trees don't belong to any lament
or any graciousness dripping from the leaves.

The windows lit our eyes. We walked at night
to see into our other lives, a table set for twelve
in one unblinking shameless picture window.
A steaming goose leapt off a platter, a knife
was buried in its back. And if we *didn't* see this happen,
neither did we expect to imagine a thing like this—
what, in the southern way, they call *thanksgivin'*,
stressing it the way they stress *um*brella, *in*surance,
putting the urgency at the front of the word,
umbrella, insurance, words held over us like thanks.
Thanks for steering the flashing cop car past us,
thanks for tucking us in like silverware folded in linen napkins.
Someone wealthy was born here, someone wealthy will die,
but let harm fly so high above these oaks tonight
it can't see down through leaves . . . and so stars flowered
down in some poorer garden wilting in the dark
between those wealthy lives and ours. It's easy now
to blame those houses for everything even they would never have.
So one rich woman sees me walking fast and calls out
your walk looks like it's going somewhere,
another woman swings open the mirrored cabinet door
of her misery and moans at me
oh lady, please come here, my teeth hurt BAD
and grinds them back and forth like china plates.
And in her sour vestibule death is not a voice
on the other end of a princess phone,
death is not crumpled tissues, death is not even a row of stars
in a phone book beside a list of doctors' names.
She doesn't die that night inside her house,
it doesn't matter what the windows want to see—
the ones across the street that stare so hungrily

into her brimming windows; even I am a window
squinting back as I pick up the phone and dial
and a doctoring voice says too familiarly
oh yes. That's Mrs. Herb. Let me talk to her.
And then, her terror mute inside my voice,
he adds, *she does this all the time. Just say*
you have to be getting home now. She'll be fine —
his weary porch-light voice shines at me
through cobweb filaments and dead black wings.
I wondered how the story would find its way
out of a house that didn't seem to live
in any neighborhood but its own dirt-poor treeless dark.
Live oak is a hard and durable wood.
Bless us, keep us, we said to the corrugations of bark.
Leave us be, to the thunderstorm foliage.
Why did they listen with only half an ear?
What did we curse with our thanks everlasting?
Above the ped-walk bridge on 59
I can still remember buckshot stars and the heavy clouds
blown inland from the Gulf of Mexico,
sucking up marsh gas and the flitterings of a cattle egret
along the way. I can smell the ocean air
and feel the half-hearted tricklings of the waves
towed in the wake of stars and clouds
departing Galveston, where sand is spotted with oil
and anyone who walks there barefoot
sooner or later feels the cold black stuff
squirt like a gritty mustard between the toes.
Three friends who used to go walking here
I've lost. And every time
death scrubbed them off the skin like squamous cells

until they *weren't*, and blackness everywhere.
But afterwards, looking back, the red brick path, the frizzy moss
escaped like strands of hair, the rippling branches,
everything, everything seems shocked to life
at the end of all twisting and turning, burnt alive at the tips
as if an errant root had lanced a wire
deep underground. Death belongs to some other story.
This one ends by night, and night is a trestle table
with a silver cloth and wistful moons for plates,
laid for twelve, though not one single guest arrives—
only the Match Girl, walking under the trees again
holding a bundle of matchsticks in her arms.
And as the night brings blackness leaf by leaf
she lights the wick of every blessed oak
then lets them burn as one great tree.

BORN WORRIER

The afghan folds around my sleeping cat, lapping her back and belly,
    all intersecting loops and openings,
        all nesting flowers brown and periwinkle blue.

I could almost believe to pluck one flower out of sleep
    begins a terrible unraveling . . .

one out of every seven people slept in the Underground,
    in London, during the blitz,
        and the other six awoke to airborne rumblings

that died in the gutters and hinges every night in September 1940 —

I am falling asleep over *Photohistory of the 20th Century,*
    snow falling through empty branches.
        Snow like a newsreel played in my head:

IN THE WINTER OF 1909, NIAGARA FALLS FROZE SOLID!
    The frozen falls looks like a stand of trees . . .

one Londoner out of seven, despite official objections.
    London Bridge Station, bombed seventeen times that year!
        as passengers to nowhere prayed to a sleep of flake and bones:

fall over us from the ceiling tiles, rise to us from the floor tiles,
    black on white on black.

*

If flesh is a bombed-out city and spirit the aftermath,
　　is light snow powdered bone and salt?
　　　　Once, in Avignon so far from ice and snow I saw,

in a glass case, bone shards: wishbone, eyelash, funny bone.

In a bedchamber at the Palace of the Popes,
　　birds on trailing vines looked down from the ceiling and walls,
　　　　an empty miter was folded across an empty bed.

Next door, in the study of Clement VI, the Chamber of the Deer,
　　I saw frescoes of stag hunts, ferret hunts, falconry.

I thought, how could anyone sleep through the din?
　　Birdcages with open doors painted in window embrasures.
　　　　How could anyone sleep through one more painted
　　　　　　tendril's hush

behind all noise, waiting for something, anything to rise?

When I was a child, Chicago lived at the end of a pointer
　　held in Khrushchev's hand. Lying in bed,
　　　　I could hear the dotted lines of my parents' late-night talk:

somewhere bombs are falling down, falling down,
　　　　shrapnel softly blizzarding over my head in the dark.

Mama used to call me a born worrier.

Sheets and blankets cold as pewter candlesticks,
      light a thumbnail under the door.

Through the window I watched snow falling out of the street light,
      watched it assemble, bone by bone, with airplane glue,
          the disembodied trees, *phalange, tarsus, metatarsal* . . .

all the bones we'd learned at school, until each tree was whole and I
  slept.

*

Sleep's at the eye of a vast impatience, though I'm not sure whose
  it is—

trains rush out of it, Omaha to Chicago, the El goes underground
      and comes up roaring into London, Victoria, Marble Arch . . .

the minute hand on the Big Ben is the size of a bus,
      St. Bride's snowy spire on Fleet Street resembles a wedding cake.
         Once from the open top of a red double-decker

I saw the half-bombed churches, the Roman statue of Lucina
      resurrected to street level because she was a goddess of light,
         stone face eaten by traffic fumes—

I could almost feel some part of her still underground, waiting for
  something;

almost asleep on the other side of a rushing train
      or a stand of frozen, circuitous trees

was the underworld, a series of black-and-white photographs,
   pictures of the frozen Niagara, pictures of bedrolls lined on
      cold cement—
         unhinged each night, a people asleep down there . . .

                                        *

. . . as I am half-asleep, looking out through remembered snowfall,
   or is it dust
      blowing back to us from the Dust Bowl days?
         Have I traveled anywhere but into this armchair?

Sleep is erasing my parents' Cold War talk, though not the cold, not
   the snow,

sleep is erasing the branches aimed at my bedroom windows,
   blind as the subterranean eyes of potatoes.
      But my childhood house is still lit inside, eternally guttering

in this book of the 20th century that I'll never get to the end of
   before sleep blows the candle out . . .

INSTRUCTIONS FOR CLEANING

I think the rain at five A.M. wants everything
back in its shadow box,
the wind, the cardinals' *what cheer*
like bits of light rubbed newsprint gray,
a nest of fine soft grasses
and human hair, a black-tailed magpie,
which, if you tame it, can imitate a human voice.
If only I could hear what it's telling me,
brush away the trees and see
what's glued to the sky,
an old French map of the universe, maybe,
Hell like a parrot's ball of cork
at the center of two revolving moons,
beyond it earth and sun, the other globes,
the stars and stars,
and outside all our orbiting
the Realm of the Happy.
Here in this cemetery it's raining
for no good reason, I hear the gravestones
sizzling like stars;
the only spot of light in all the universe
is a single porch light, the caretaker's cottage.
It travels toward me unsteadily,
smearing itself on tree trunks
that get in the way.
Moisten windows of Castle
by breathing on them wrote Cornell,
instructions for cleaning one of his boxes,
but if I blew on a cottage window,
what in all tarnation would I see—
the three bright stars of the Summer Triangle,

Vega, Deneb, Altair?
Only in a shadow box
whose stars are flecks or streaks of paint
or bird shit running down the midnight blue
behind a cage's broken wire mesh,
the parrot flown . . . .
Maybe the parting of married friends
is a light switched on and off
in a house where nobody lives.
I remember seeing the one friend's hand
travel slowly up the wall
to my print drawer to touch some tiny object there,
trying to be so careful,
knocking a lump of coral out of its niche
while the other friend gathered
their daughter up in a blanket
so as not to lose any part of her,
arm or leg, to the cold.
Now in a summer of constant rain,
what if I plucked a hidden chickadee
out of the minuscule path of its falling
feebee, would the sadness hiss out like a match?
Would the rain stop falling
or would it fall up into the trees
like friends coming home to each other?
Lights are going on
in houses all along the edge of the cemetery,
but the cottage windows are dark
as if what holds the stones together now
is rain, all light having drained away
like a battery dead overnight.

It happens fast, it seems
to the ones outside
who breathe on the windows to moisten them.

III

ON THE PHONE WITH MY PARENTS

I didn't know there could be so many silences
listening in on our conversation,
or having their own conversations

like sleepless passengers in a row,
vapors of mingling
gin and vermouth above each empty

plastic airline cup in business class.
Silences cut in and out
along with the phantom voices that sometimes haunt my line:

Panda Bear,
are you stopping in Kalamazoo?
Not on your life. Radiation

has certain side effects. That's all my father says
on bad days,
and who knows how far he's traveled

just to get to our conversation.
He used to travel a lot on business,
and when he came home from New York or Chicago,

part of him seemed missing
less precisely than the Arrow shirts or sock cocoons
entombed in the suitcase lost by TWA.

Lately he's home whenever I call.
My mother's voice is a bright pool
sailboats knife across but

motors aren't allowed to mar.
Like me, she thinks in metaphor: if she slipped
out of focus, she might be a marsh,

treeless, periodically inundated.
Their side of the conversation floats up the West Coast
all the way to Alaska

and passes so close to the hull of a glacier
the cruise director hauls up a bucketful of ice.
Drinks for everyone.

There's that fruity smell of gin and lime,
and the fathomless tinkling of their glasses
drives itself into the icy trees,

the ones on my side, landlocked Kalamazoo,
where snow is falling fast and thick,
pouring out of the very street light

as if it wanted to bury this town.

OF THE CONSTELLATION PERSEUS

My father's den has a wraparound stereo sound,
speakers fore and aft, every way you turn
    there's Natalie Cole's aquatic
Mona Lisa pouring its vacancies
over her father's dead voice, or is it
    into his dead ear? Of course
my father's ear is alive
to the many distances invented between us
    like stereo channels:
channel one is a tidal voice in your ear,
channel two, not one voice but a concert hall's
    murmuring heart. If I could listen preternaturally
to my father's heart, I wouldn't
want to hear the little lag or leap,
    the abnormality found by a recent EKG,
what either makes him tick
or frets away at him because, it don't take much:
    after all, in the Perseid meteor shower
each shooting star you see is a grain
of interplanetary dust
    ablaze in the wake of the comet Swift-Tuttle,
last seen in the 19th century.
So were Tuttle and Swift.
    As for me, I was always the last girl awake
at a Girl Scout camp-out, in a fenced backyard I lay
at the end of a row of bedrolls
    shapeless as cat mummies.
Here and there a star petered out,
but a conversational glow hung over two lawn chairs,
    the troop leader and her husband,
whose red-tipped cigarettes reigned over

my almost-sleep. On the pure puffed thought
        of a feather pillow I glutted myself
while inside the hem of my flashlight beam
Jim told Huck a shooting star
        is an egg hove out of the nest,
and the river lazied them south
past the snuffed houses of Cairo.

LAKES

A garden glove so far away
I have to look through the wrong end of a telescope.
Then I see
the thumb and forefinger are busted out
as if too many times
my father'd flashed the OK sign at me
across the roses he was dusting white
or over a bucket of withering dandelions.
Inside that glove
all motion stops, or did it blow away
on a wind that glances off the water
and sways a neighbor's dock
so rowboats bump and clang together
like a row of dusty bells?
A man in a Sunfish
is waving to someone: me?
Across this man-made lake
some idiot dyed bright blue,
the windows are a dying glimpse of sky,
a great blue heron folds its long neck
and flaps away, then circles back
as if it doesn't matter
where it settles, every cattail clutter
looks the same
because a glinting jet trail's told
how late it is high over the roofs.
Nearby at the Barrington Jewel-Osco
a flock of teenage herring gulls
mistook the parking lot for open water
fifty miles from Lake Michigan . . .
hot afternoons, they soar above the grocery carts

on waves of rising air.
I ask them how can anyone
stand to live out here,
South Barrington, cul-de-sacs
like rootless lily pads
on a treeless lake, houses with circular drives
and double doors like funeral parlors.
On the heap of sand-and-pebble beach
I can turn and see
my parents' newish clapboard house
inside its paperweight,
so tiny I could pick it up in my hand
and peer in its windows,
or pull out all the straight pins
that hold it together, or even
unravel the spider's silver spittle
gluing chimney brick to brick. Anything
could shake that house apart,
the tail-flick of a male robin,
the line of mud on the female's breast
as she thrusts and shapes
the cup of her nest.
And if the single garden glove
could tug at the Chinese elm
and earth and sky began to tip,
wouldn't the tree give way
with all its crumbly roots
and fall into the sky?
Robins flourish everlastingly in suburbs,
hopping the prolific grass,
stopping to peck, to lift and swallow,

foraging their shadows
then flying away with them.
And I suspect the lake
of dreaming too of flight,
overrunning its shores toward the Great Lakes,
drowning every house on the way
to Lake Michigan,
where lately, fifteen miles offshore,
divers discovered a field of tree stumps
eighty-five feet deep,
traces of oak and ash trees that stood
eight thousand years ago
at the edge of what was then
a much smaller lake.
Maybe the point
of man-made lakes so far inland
is to give back a center.
Years ago my parents moved away,
or maybe the shore got turned around
and we were lost
from all those houses looking over the lake
waiting for trees
to come out of the water
and take them back.

MORBID

Neither the mailboxes nor the windows would tell me
how much love was mine
as the houses walked me home from school.

Gold and silver numbers nailed to the houses
were practical stars, but did anyone care?

I wasted a lot of time and lust back then
on thoughts of Jesus, stars, dead birds, the back of the head
and the cinder-block shoulders of Marty DiPrimo

one desk away from my fingertips if I should dare

but sold and gone by sooty after-school autumn dusk
and moody afternoon TV.

I used to scribble assassination haiku in study hall.

Friday night was rumors, car keys, seat belts, bra straps slipping
     down.
Egg and tomato splatted on fence boards,
toilet paper pennants strung from trees.

Lips and shadow, tampon holders, orchids pining, tongue on
     tongue.

But Friday night Jo Ellen Donatelli, black-haired greaser girl
who *had* a boyfriend, Carl,
swallowed a bottle of sleeping pills and did it, really, died—

all week in school, thoughts of armholes
of her sleeveless sweater spooling under her arms

gave camera shots: white bra, sculptured armpit. Almost home

my house pinned aimlessly to its *1720*
was already hunkering down in shame at what would be

the used-up flame of Friday night.
I'd watch the TV late shows, midnight, three A.M., beyond all
   curfews,
taste of kiss in my throat

and lungs and down the muscle fibers to my fingertips,

where God was microscopic cells and I was afraid
of the numberless houses
I could find in the dark.

OLD THINGS

Each newborn pink adobe house believes its summer moon
has been dead for weeks. It sends its cold light
mercifully down to us in the oven-dark
so each house lives until morning on a puff of refrigerated air.
Then the scorpions crawl back into their holes
and the black widow spiders lay their red spots down in the dust.
My mother's knuckles used to thicken and ache when it rained
but now she lives where it never rains:
she and my father sit on their patio wistfully, watching for clouds
to rise like cartoon thought-bubbles above the golf course.
Clouds hover over the mountains ringing
the greater Phoenix-and-Scottsdale metropolitan area
but don't stray much from the cities or spawn of the cities:
houses backing away from an epicenter of skyscrapers,
outlying cul-de-sacs, swimming pools like a handful of magic beans.
Jellied colonies lopsiding out toward Buckeye and Carefree,
Squaw Peak and the Superstitions, toward the tenth year of my life
and the two sprawled bodies found near the Eye of the Needle:
two young men fallen out of the pockets of death
on their search for the Lost Dutchman's Mine.
The evening news, I remember, got the story wrong at first—
the men were found hungry but alive, reported the anchorman,
and the wives in front of their televisions heard the news.
For how many minutes, those lost men powered on joy and reproach,
oh my god you gave us such a scare!
until the ringing of telephones followed us out of the past,
until silence on the other end of the line was the absence of hunger.
Until a voice spoke out of each dead mouth
and told the waiting houses there is nothing out there
that won't keep company with spider mites and dust.

*

Was history never a series of wistful afternoons,
figure eights and petal stitch on curtains
passing one shade on to another?
The time it takes to lick my forefinger and turn a page
is almost enough for the page to have yellowed
and passed from "collectible" to "antique"—
to have traveled the distance from what makes me feel old
to what makes my parents feel old.

                              No distance at all
from the striped barber's pole on the corner of childhood
to the thought *what a quaint old town!*

And see how I can't help but simplify all our childhoods to a
     single past?
The book I'm paging through is *San Francisco's Great Disaster: A Full
     Account
of the Recent and Terrible Destruction of Life and Property, 1906,*
bought in an antique shop along with a foldout paper fan
with a two-digit phone number printed on the back
under ROYAL AMBULANCE AND FUNERAL SERVICE—
let's call that bored little town
that dreamed up fires and earthquakes and injury and death
and warn it: save us a street here and there for the smaller tragedies,
save the street signs that tell us where we are,
save the wooden numbers nailed to the trees
and a few clapboard houses to sway like willows in the aftershock.

*

Time is starting to bloom at the knuckle,

this arthritic index finger mine, this ache,
this humid, used-up, gray midwestern town.
I live in a house that's older than my parents are
but my grown-up brother and sister and I
will be children
as long as parents stand at the door of a house
on the golf course edging the suburbs of anywhere.

They wave us back into the past,
where our Beatles Flip Your Wig game is new in its box
and marbles bulge from a knotted argyle sock
darned at heel and toe.
My favorite marble is still the blue one swirled with white
like the planet earth,
my favorite toy a china JFK
perched on a saltshaker chair, three holes for pepper
drilled between his shoulder blades
like an awful joke on time and kitsch.

My mother picks him up and shakes him
over a peeled hard-boiled egg
then sets him back on his throne,
too early, or is it already too late?
He isn't born yet and he isn't dead,
tiny king of a town I barely remember.

*

Once I watched a non-event on film—
a sticky afternoon, a black-and-white New Jersey afternoon
in 1953. A child slowly pedaled his tricycle down a sidewalk
that square by square renewed itself

so he never got where we thought he was going.
A woman bent her body right down to the end of the world
and poured an impure quiet out of a watering can.
Twice that evening, time would stop
being anyone's father and mother, time would be so hungry it
  would gorge itself
on the bodies of Ethel and Julius Rosenberg,
carve them out and leave their children dark and ravening inside.
Nothing happened to that dead New Jersey hour
but a child's wondering as he pedaled nowhere—
what were the ancient stains hidden under the antimacassar on
  the sofa at home?
what was the darkness leaking out of every eye of the eyelet
  tablecloth
draping the drop-leaf mahogany dining room table?
Who'd bring a wood that dark into the world?

Childhood must have started sometime before his parents' births
and centuries after mine.
Out of its quiet streets came the end of its history.

My parents live on the edge of the desert without a past
except the one they make by switching lights on and off.
Their lights are set on timers when nobody's home.
And isn't this a kind of history barging around in the dark,
their dark or anyone's, made of burnt matches, dead batteries,
  and used-up bulbs,
trying, preposterously, to come up with a lighted window?
As a child, I lived in a house on a cul-de-sac
with my mother and father and sister and brother.
My mother used to tell us she was sweet sixteen

and I thought how sweet and long a teenage life could be.
On weekends she and my father would shop for furniture
and drag us kids along to Ethan Allen or Sears.
We trailed through phony bedrooms and kitchens and living
     rooms
and thought ourselves inside a house with invisible walls,
a house so big we might never see each other again
and after an hour we hoped we never would.
We'd stand at the wall of glowing doorbells wired to ring,
and we'd ring and ring them with our prodding imperious
     fingers
and drive our parents mad:
boredom demanding a thousand doors to let it out.
If the doors had opened, wouldn't the neighborhoods we've
     invented
look like the shiny pages of *San Francisco's Great Disaster*,
the twisted streetcar tracks and the birdcage city hall
and the rain of brick and plaster mingled with bone?

And the streets deserted.
Whoever it was played there before us
still sleeps through town after town as the earth
like an old tin locomotive rides us all down mangled tracks,
past rocking skyscrapers and clapboard bungalows,
the golf course and the outpost Circle K
until there is no town and no jumping off.

THE PELICAN GIRL

His voice is dreamy, saying her name.
Sometimes don't we talk that way
about the old loves, the lost ones?
Said as if parting had charmed her life:
that Pelican girl,
named like one in a fairy tale bewitched at dawn,
awakening to a fish-light polish
along her spooning bill and a newly hopeful
boat-shaped buoyancy. Later the townsfolk,
whose eyes are idle glimmerings,
will search the waves for her human body
as pelicans plunge and scoop
and her happiness opens out like wingspread
soundlessly over the rooftops
as if it were trying not to wake them.

The rest of the story has to do with her falling in love
with a rooster weather vane and its turning away
with every puff of wind.

On the shore of Superior north of Duluth, it is early summer
     again,
but down at the lake bottom
it must have been winter always.
I saw my first pelicans there,
bobbing far out on the waves like volleyballs
from a game played on an ice floe . . .
I didn't like thinking how cold they had to be
not to feel such cold.
We were camped illegally in a forest
as dark and circuitous as a witch's shriek,

our orange pup tent wedged between trees,
tiny lick of a flame,
and one flame's warmth was all we could summon
out of a camp stove as big as two fists.
Even the freeze-dried hash had a savor
of tin and kryptonite.
In the middle of night (where trespassing is forbidden)
we thought we heard someone walking around the tent,
not a raccoon or a bear but a human, circling.
Every footstep carried a heavy *thunk*.

My dreams took over with someone pounding his fists
on the ripstop walls of the tent,
then turned oblique,
he and I were climbing upstairs to bed
in my childhood house on Forest Lane, but it had no upper
    floor.
When I woke, it was black and deep,
and morning had floated out
to the middle of Lake Superior.
Neither of us could help the other
except by living through the story
that ended the summer,
and our tent was eaten by battery acid.
When back at home we unfolded it from the trunk,
it looked like a giant burning snowflake
cut out by the child in both of us
if the child were Charles Manson.

Imagine a storm full of snowflakes like that,
falling into Superior, burning,

sizzling out in the world's deepest lake.
And if our voices are dreamy
when we speak of the lost world,
the charmed lives, the girl who stitched a shirt
out of stinging nettles without complaint,
the boy who wore it minus a sleeve
so his arm was a swan's wing,
still we have found and kept each other whole
as they could not.

AUTISTIC TWINS AT THE FIREWORKS

They see, directly, a universe and a heaven
of numbers.
              —Oliver Sacks, "The Twins"

We're sorry we put no stock in you or your homemade stars,
the stink of your cherry bombs, your ash-worms toiling out of
    pellets,
your territorial picnic blankets engulfing the continents of your
    arms and legs,

the sparklers you think will pay your way into heaven's parking lot,
the oohs and ahs when language blanks you out
and you see each burst of sparks in its instant, unmediated,

as we, you think, must see. What are we doing here?
Autistics. Half-wits. Morons. Angels. Idiot savants.

Words, like the vanishings you have come out to celebrate.

They end where the numbers begin.
Give us a date forty thousand years into the future or past
and we'll tell you in unison what day of the week it was or will
    be evermore.

We *know* that day. We've seen its face.
We've seen the faces of numbers.

I'll say a number, he'll say it back to me with a musing smile,
tasting, groping all the way to its depths or his or mine,
what is the difference, what do we care,

our black thick glasses magnify our eyes,
our heads are huge and bobbing on our silly chicken necks.
You are the dots in a connect-the-dots picture for children.

We'd like to but we can't connect the dots, or care for them,
for you, your faces, voices, jerry-built or real.

No number would rent out the emptiness of your faces tonight.

Each firecracker eats away at you, each bottle rocket eats away at the
    dark
but the dark is too great to digest.
You ride on your blankets as if you could ride past the dark and
    the waiting.

The real stars are cold and dead like the tips of your fingers.
When you touch us, your skin is as real as the north celestial pole.

Like trained bears the attendant led us into the Quik-Stop for candy
and the face behind the counter looked across at us
with two looks, one, two, as if we were twin beds

or a right and left boxing hook.
And she said to me, "When you look in the mirror, do you get
    confused?"
And she said to him, "Are you you or your twin?"

We smiled back at the lips and the wafting of eyelashes.
Come outside, they said. Live in the world.

But the world is sly.

While the face was busy talking, the bottles stacked behind it
had changed into a number
indivisible by anything but itself and one.

And as a friend it spoke to us, and in us, and out of every label
  and every face.

EVERLASTINGS

for my mother

The name is so hopeful, what we call
little bundles of flowers you've hung upside down in the kitchen
until they look like equal parts
of stars and rust.

For me they radiate a tension
felt by finger and thumb at the edge of a page —
flowers you'd see by the side of a road
between the towns of Here and Gone,

where the families in photographs live
in houses whose boards are the color of cuttlefish ink.
Thrust of a daylily through a broken fence
and the mint leaves worming their way across a yard

where your husband-to-be in a navy uniform pieced out of the dark,
his sailor hat bulging out at the sides like a rope-ladder pie,
stands by a fat man in a pin-striped suit;
their elbows touch: they're father-and-son.

If hope springs eternal, why not dried flowers, why not
the fathers-and-sons and the reticence
that has hyphenated them,
why not the trees and the silences that accumulate

between gone days, why not the houses and trees slipped out of
    their colors
and into the sadder, more angular

black and gray and brownish inks long dried on paper?
Aeternus, past and future, what is the difference,

son into husband, trees into reticence,
petals sweetening on their way to dust or wherever they're going,
not there yet, not even gone —
these roses, statice, broods of sunflowers —

you on the piano, playing minor chords to suit
a moody daughter's silences, the trees.

I V

A NIGHT WITHOUT STARS

And the lake was a dark spot
                 on a lung.
Some part of its peace was dead; the rest was temporary. Sleeping
  ducks and geese,
goose shit underfoot
               and wet gray blades of grass.
The fingerlings like sleeping bullets
                    hung deep in the troughs of the hatchery
and cold traveled each one end to end,
such cold,
     such distances.

We lay down in the grass on our backs—
beyond the hatchery the streetlights were mired in fog and so
there were no stars,
        or stars would say there was no earth.

Just a single homesick firefly lit on a grass blade.
Just our fingers
       curled and clutching grass,
this dark our outmost hide, and under it
                  true skin.

ABSENT BIRD MOON

After the thunder moon and the green corn moon
there is no moon at all in the autumn rain

unless the moon is made of mud and feathers,
cat hair, pencil shavings, fern, and thistledown,

unless the moon is a nest in a barren tree,
hollow inside where a hand or bird would fit,

cold and gray and empty of birds.
But I don't know what to call this. Rain moon. Absent bird moon.

Gray squirrel dead on its back in the road again moon.
Nothing, born each second and hung by its thread,

so what do we do if the moons escape,
do we drown in the ocean of yellow leaves?

Would it give us something to talk about?
All those leaves brushing different windows on my face

until I feel like the windows without the house
or the missing ideogram for *falling leaf,*

the word we don't have in English another window, clear and blank.
And when I breathe on it, nothing, not even fog.

My husband misremembered the word for *toothbrush* one morning
as *toothbride.* In the rain, his umbrella was a *rainbow.*

Moon, why can't you see how meaning drifts to its leaf, as I see
the Pizza Hut on the corner is a ruby awake all night?

All night delivery cars rev up like heartburn.
There I am at the window again, and what I hear

has a sort of a name: the *caw* of a crow, and another, another.
So high I barely see them flying over the house.

One night I found my grandmother crouched on the stairwell,
     listening
to her son, my father; his wife, her daughter-in-law,

my mother, below in the den. What a cast of characters
for just two little tireless talking mouths.

Words I think were dissolving like ice cubes in a glass.
I think by then she had hardening of the arteries,

veins inside the woody tissue of her legs had lignified
to xylem, tracheids, pitted cell walls, fiber.

I can't figure out what they're talking about.
I stood beside her and we made no sound,

as if we had turned into trees and were listening
to a *caw caw caw* blowing over the leaves.

So tonight a leaf rides upstairs on the mud on my shoe.
When I lift my foot, I see the leaf, when I peel it off

I see in mud the ghost of that leaf.
Where does the leaf go? If we are the trees

and there is no moon, then how do we ferry
black specks of birds back down to their actual size?

JOY TO THE WORLD

Why I hate to be up in the air,
dangling in a car on a wire strung between two alps
above the village of Chamonix,
is not that much of a puzzle.
I'm afraid the thread will snap, we'll drop
and smash apart like a music box—
the one I had when I was four, with its painted lid,
a snowy glacier winding around a tiny Swiss chalet
as if to tuck it in. When I lifted the lid,
the whirring butterfly gears played a muted song
I thought of as *Joy to the World* (not the Christmas tune)
because those words made me want to cry,
lying under the covers in late afternoon,
watching the honeyed light brim up in the globes of my eyes
so they wouldn't see sleep coming out of the mountains.
A woman swallows and clenches the handrail
but does this quietly, to herself, as if her fear
were something small and tightly wound
and she wouldn't want it played to the other two of us.
As for myself, I concentrate on looking out, not down,
as if we were thousands of miles from earth,
as if this deep into space we have left behind even nostalgia.
As if is the motor that hums and carries us
from the lower peak to the higher
in forty thousand hammering breaths,
and all our reasons—Bill's, the woman's, mine—for braving this
    height
shape into tremendous peaks on the other side of the valley,
and, highest of all, Mont Blanc—
what a friend pronounces *Mount Blank* and we always laugh,
but what I see now is tremendously blank,

what burns in my eyes when I look at something that white,
what chafes my sweaty palms when I think of anything that high.
Just for an instant I feel it, the white, taking everything back,
even words: nothing's been said or ever will be.
Like pages of memory, language is waiting
for something to happen, the slightest change on the slopes
or in the clouds shaping over them.
Then the light backs off, or maybe my eyes adjust
and words streak over our silences
like the fissures we see carved into glacial ice
that, deep underneath, is Windex-blue.
But all along I hated the thought of having to ride back down—
I think that is part of the dread:
some of the whiteness rides down too, like a paper cut.
We have the swaying car to ourselves this time
and so I can't help it, I let go and cry.
And the woman who doesn't ride down with us,
maybe she wants to be alone on the wobbly *téléphérique,*
holding her body as rigid inside her clothes
as the gods in their marble skin on the grounds of Versailles,
or the dog I see a few days later in a still life by Chardin,
poised on the verge of upsetting the polished fruit.
Later, in Paris, that woman seems almost a part of history:
Marie Antoinette wandering inside her tiny 18th century
prison yard of remaining life, stroking the edge of a grass blade,
the way we tease ourselves with the future;
the Mona Lisa, whose skin has a radioactive glow . . .
we spend one afternoon among pendulous roses grown for a
    royal party,
the little nothings trained into trees of perfumed breath
we breathe as we walk up and down the rows,

having driven here through the moving parking lots of Paris,
where at least we are close to the ground.
On the flight home, dosed with Xanax, I miss the northern lights
or almost miss them, lifting my heavy head
to blow a vaporous rose on the little window
that blanks out forever the ravening flickers of green.
Then sleep snows me over and I'm not there or even here
in the empty universe that, after Mont Blanc,
can't think of anything else to invent but death.

EXAM

Had any children? the doctor asks. I say *No.*
And close my lips—the other half of the answer.
If this were a party, I'd feel I had to go on,
even if the other person hadn't asked
Why not? or *Are you planning on having any?*
They feel free to ask. And almost always, I explain
something about wanting them but not enough,
or how I wish I had two lives: in one of them
I'd have a child by now. But it's no good,
not doing something never sounds as real
as doing it. I seem to stand in for reserve,
my life a keeping back, a state of being
not in active service. But I meant to talk here about time,
the way it passes us at different rates,
two people in the same room—parent and non-parent,
or doctor and patient in an examining room
just big enough for a desk, a table, and a curtain between them,
quite a squeeze with the nurse. For me, the moment has slowed
to simple sentences in present tense.
He asks. I answer. I lie back. She comes in.
They look inside. I answer. No one asked.
For him, the moment probably speeds along,
a paragraph of questions, then another paragraph
of looking with a flashlight. Then
a paragraph of silent writing down.
This doctor doesn't say much with his face.
I'm worried, he's evasive. It's his job
to stay just out of reach.
And crazily, there comes into my head
a job interview I was on once, in a hotel room,
a row of professors sitting on a bed.

One of them smiles and asks me, *Why do **you** think*
so many fiction writers use the present tense these days?
Some answer that the teaching job depends on
hangs in a cloud of thought inside his head.
I can't think, I make something stupid up.
Maybe I should have told him I was terrified
to find myself in that moment, present tense,
stuck in a simple sentence, having to ride it out
by talking and gesturing, hearing my voice in my ears,
which sounds like it doesn't know what it thinks
it's talking about, and my hands move awkwardly
inside the gloves of hands.
I think that man despised the present tense,
and the fiction writers who those days were using it,
despised the short-sightedness of the moment,
any foolish groping in a tiny dark.
I close my eyes and still feel this cold table,
long as my life, and the doctor is gone
except for his gloved hands and the ice-cold
unseen instrument holding me open,
gone the ceiling and walls, just me and the table,
me inside the top half of my clothes,
bra and over it the blouse buttoned up to the top
to keep me safe at home,
and the opening of me between my legs
and the tiny beam of the flashlight
he plays around in me. He's in the dark too,
I guess—he just moves through it faster.
You're probably fine, but let's have an X ray just in case—
make sure nothing sinister's going on.
He smiles a little then, to soften the *sinister*

or maybe just downshifting for an instant
into his natural personality.
As for me, I don't understand anything about time,
how it passes from your parents into you
then into your children, if you have any,
or where it goes to if you don't.
Keep me going, doc, I almost say.
And don't say, but he knows. And God knows what, inwardly,
    he answers.
Then his smile vanishes, it is no longer possible.
He draws the curtain around me,
I put on the bottom half of my clothes,
trying to rustle as little as I can
while, on the other side, he goes and sits down at his desk
and writes, I can *hear* it, another paragraph:
my paragraph. The one I'm rushing through.

WIND

—Zennor, Cornwall, September 1995

Poor geese, riled up by something they can't see—
a movement and a force, a presence that betrays
so much of itself, so little of anything
it spooks me. And sends geese shrieking in a herd
across the muddy grass and back again,
led by the dirty-looking gander always in charge
of a universal silliness and panic.
They look to me like the forerunners of birds
seen from a distance, figures on a plain,
awkward, huge at the lonely end of perspective—
their wings, still at the blueprint stage,
splayed back and flapping uselessly behind,
won't function for another billion years.
Still, with huffed-up feathers and the scared, thrust-forward squeals,
the panic they create is up-to-date
and feels human. That, at least, is how I see it,
since history is the course of *human* events,
not how a wind spooked geese or dinosaurs
but how it blasts against the face
of our graves and monuments and wears us down
in a time too big for us to know.
Or want to know. I hoped for dreams last night,
but they won't come just because you want them to.
I wanted some image, some juxtaposition or incongruity
to bear a little mystery:
at home my brother's lover lies in a coma
both deeper and shallower than sleep.
The wind could rant and storm all night,
it wouldn't wake him up

or tell us just exactly where he's gone. . . . *This godforsaken place*
is how the car mechanic, called from town, describes it out here.
Said with loathing and a kind of pride:
he's lived around here all his life,
not just the easy summer season but the winters,
which take *years*. That word an inkling only
of what is going to come, what everyone who lives here
talks about to strangers, tourists, my husband and me.
Just mention winter, and you'll hear the wind,
the word itself, and something behind the word,
I'm not sure what. September
and already I have lain awake
as wind howls out the shape of the house.
I have heard the roof and walls struggle to form.
Already something in me is lying down
as the browned ferns lie down now across the moors.
The mechanic thinks we're crazy to have come.
He is missing a tooth in front —
the look of it goes with the dire quality of his voice
and the dark stains up and down his coveralls.
He bends over our sterile cough of a car,
the door of its chest opened wide to the world.
I ask him *will it make it through winter?*
but hold the other question back: *will we?*
Under the touch of his fingers on the HT leads
my husband and I float helplessly . . .
strong winds, frail walls. Back home
Tom is ebbing into his death, my mother says,
like the Cheshire cat. Into nothingness, with a smile
left brooding. Then not even that.
That stupid squawking of geese —

hee-yah as close to words as I can bring the sound—
is as good a vocalization as any
for living in this place, or for the force of wind
trying to blow us right out of our bodies.
Geese must feel that too. Why else are they running,
if not to catch up with that rush
of trying to stay exactly where you are?

SPOOKED

The geese are little lighthouses
shining into everything
with their squawks, black light
of horse manure, the rasp of gorse,
the galloping away
of the spooked hills. Maybe it is a muteness
in their clipped wings
that drives them to frenzy,
the inability to fly
is what's honking and gabbling into the silences
of things that never stir,
as if an earthly racket loud enough
were a kind of flight. To me
it feels exactly like gravity, that ruckus
weighs me down to earth.
The loudest, biggest goose is the oldest, 27 years.
I swear that when he looks at me
I'm just a tiny noise.
He looks a little crazy, staring hard,
like he could fly right out of me.
This morning I heard a bellowing,
full blast, within a barn.
A cow that wanted out,
wanted it over and over
until the longing to get outside
was bigger than the barn
and offered no way out.
I couldn't possibly own up to it,
that hopeless hope —
not even in my wet boots
caked with mud and shit.

I had to believe a human hope more intricate,
with doors and windows
and a roof that lifted off.
Climbing over a stile, I felt myself traveling
above the mud and stone, as light and time,
but then my boots set down on grass again
and me squarely inside.

SAD BEAUTY

At twilight, when I walk the neighbor's dog
through fields of mangled cow-shit blossoms
down to the sea, the bushes jump at our approach,
a hare leaps out and sprints away,
vanished almost before the leap begins
to register. This happens again and again.
And every time it does I can believe
in the changing light, trust
passage is that easy, things begin
and end in each other wholly and naturally,
bush to rabbit, rabbit to air,
and thus fulfill themselves.
A process with no memory of beginning and end.
But this shy old gentleman greyhound knows
something still partly rabbit in the air,
tastes or smells some trace of blood or breath . . .
and yearns against obedience
into an even longer, thinner dog—
wanting so hugely to be gone,
he's not so much a dog as a flickering.
A dog that doesn't need a leash.
You can tell he was beaten by somebody habitually—
the way he'll visit, suddenly just *there,*
having stepped inside your door
and standing now with four white paws
exactly on the rug, irresolute, a glide
about to rush back out or stretch
his legs into a lying down that ends
just where your patience ends.
Begins with this dog
and ends at such sad beauty.

Basho found it
in the morning glory
even when it's painted badly.
Today a mist hangs low over the world
from my cottage window, Bronze Age stone walls
crisscross up and over the hills
and I wonder where they are taking us.
Forward or back?
Curves of the road from Zennor to St. Ives
that show up in the mist
are getting nowhere, one by one—no bus on Sunday.
So many people live here without cars,
no one getting anywhere,
the story stays exactly where it was
on dreary days
three or four thousand years ago.
The Bronze Age. Yellow flowers
bloom across the moors
and shine even through mist,
as if the sun could force its way to earth
through dark green, sharp-tongued gorse.
A little frightening, that passage into speech,
the yellow
not acting docile as it would
on sunny days. Yesterday it was sunny—
from this porch I could see
practically to infinity, where, on a hill,
a tiny coffee-colored cow, cut out
exactly with a pair of manicure scissors,
grazed on a field of golf-course green.
Sometimes I wonder about those

Bronze Age Sundays, or days when nothing helps,
and you know the gale winds and standing stones
are interchangeable,
call and response, whisper and listening,
and you know the end's the beginning,
a pair of crows
atop the first stone wall—
the first and last thing you can see from here.
The intermingling and the passage.

About the Verna Emery Poetry Prize

Named after the retired Purdue University Press managing editor committed to developing and nurturing contemporary poetry, the Verna Emery Poetry Prize competition invites writers to submit unpublished book-length collections of original poems. The competition is open to all poets. If you would like more information and submission guidelines on the Verna Emery Poetry Prize, please send a self-addressed stamped envelope to:

Verna Emery Poetry Prize
1532 South Campus Courts, Building E
West Lafayette, Indiana 47907-1532

Winners of the Verna Emery Poetry Prize

Christianne Balk, *Desiring Flight*
Richard Cecil, *Alcatraz*
Fleda Brown Jackson, *Do Not Peel the Birches*
Lucia Perillo, *The Body Mutinies*
Donald Platt, *Fresh Peaches, Fireworks, & Guns*

Available from Purdue University Press, 1-800-933-9637